Quiz # 125702
Book Level: 2.3
Points: 5

Published in the United States in 1987 by
Franklin Watts, 387 Park Avenue South, New York, NY10016

© Aladdin Books Ltd

Designed and produced by
Aladdin Books Ltd, 70 Old Compton Street, London W1

ISBN 0 531 17071 3
Library of Congress
Catalog Card No 87 80451

Printed in Belgium

First timers

THE NEW BABY

KATE PETTY
and
LISA KOPPER

Franklin Watts
New York · London · Toronto · Sydney

Sam's Mom has got a very big stomach.
Sam can't sit on her lap now.
"Never mind," says Mom,
"I won't be like this for much longer."

Sam leans against Mom instead
and they make themselves comfortable.
He feels the baby kicking inside her.
Perhaps the baby enjoys stories too!

Mom gets things ready for the baby.
"Was I ever this little?" asks Sam.
"Yes," says Mom, "I'll find some photos
of you when you were tiny."

Sam laughs. "Wasn't I funny?"
"Little babies are often funny.
I expect this baby will make you laugh
sometimes," says Mom.

Dad is taking Mom to the hospital
because the baby is ready to be born.
Dad calls Sam's friends
and they come to take him to the park.

When Sam gets home, Granny's there
to give him his supper.
Granny lets him skip his bath tonight
and doesn't mind if he stays up late!

"Wake up, Sam!" Dad hasn't slept at all.
"You've got a baby sister!" says Dad.
"We think we'll call her Jenny.
How do you like that name?"

They stop for presents on the way
to the hospital. "Hurry up, Sam,
Mom's waiting." Sam chooses a panda
for the baby and some flowers for Mom.

At the hospital they go up in an elevator.
Sam can hear the newborn babies
as soon as the doors open.

"Where's the baby?" She's just waking up.
Sam gazes at his tiny new sister.
She's very small and rather wrinkled.
"Hello Jenny," says Sam.

Today they bring Mom and Jenny home.
Sam is glad to have Mom back.
He's looking forward
to showing Jenny his things.

But Jenny goes straight to bed.
So does Mom! Dad is busy
so Sam helps himself to a drink. Oh no!
Dad decides it's time for a cuddle!

Jenny keeps Mom and Dad very busy.
She needs to be bathed . . . and changed . . .
and fed . . . and changed again.
Sometimes they wish she'd go to sleep.

Jenny has lots of visitors.
She has lots of presents too.
They don't always make her happy.
But presents always cheer Sam up!

Jenny is dressed to go out today.
Sam and Dad are taking her for a walk.
Be careful with the carriage!
It's hard work getting it down the steps.

The neighbors stop to look at the baby.
Sam feels quite proud of her.
Sam pushes the carriage. Jenny falls asleep.
Well done, Sam.

Sam talks to Jenny as Dad changes her.
She watches him all the time.
Sam laughs at the funny faces she makes.
It's her bedtime at last.

"Come and sit on my lap, Sam," says Mom.
Sam can't imagine life without Jenny
but just now it's nice to have Mom
all to himself again.

cuddling

Mom and baby

crying

rattle

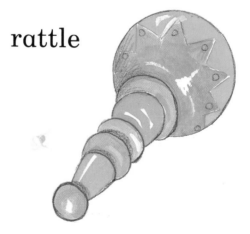

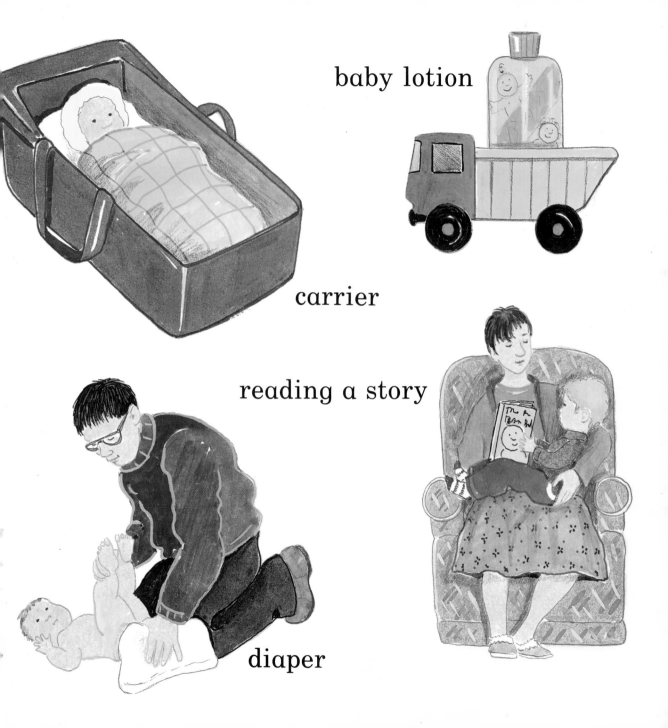

baby lotion

carrier

reading a story

diaper